THE ART POEMS
AMANDA BINTU HOLIDAY

Published by Akashic Books
©2018 Amanda Bintu Holiday

ISBN: 978-1-61775-629-0

Printed in China through Four Colour Print Group, Louisville, Kentucky
First printing

Akashic Books
Brooklyn, New York, USA
Ballydehob, Co. Cork, Ireland
Twitter: @AkashicBooks
Facebook: AkashicBooks
E-mail: info@akashicbooks.com
Website: www.akashicbooks.com

African Poetry Book Fund
Prairie Schooner
University of Nebraska
110 Andrews Hall
Lincoln, Nebraska 68588

TABLE OF CONTENTS

(Most of these poems are inspired by artworks, details of which can be found in the acknowledgments.)

PREFACE
by Kayombo Chingonyi

Much has been made, in the history of literary criticism, about the relationship between poetry and music. So rich is this kinship that there is an argument for figuring poetry as a kind of verbal music. What becomes clear upon reading Amanda Bintu Holiday's *The Art Poems* is that the sound of a poem is only one of the ways that it generates meaning. What is particularly striking about these poems is the manner in which they carry an image whole into the reader's mind. Take "The Blue Pot," for example, which—by the dint of its brevity—bears quotation in full:

> How the old man ran
> with his belly out
> and a spindly cane
> and a big blue pot
> pressed on his head
> and his barky dog
> atop the lot.

This poems feels emblematic of Holiday's wider project, insomuch as the story, such as it is, is completed in the reader's mind. The poem is deliberately unresolved, or unresolvable, at the level of referential meaning, and yet it carries significance. The reason for this is that it is an extended hand; an invitation to enter with the poet into a process of imagination. That there is a work of visual art that sparked this poem only serves to extend this feeling of a leap into the imaginative realm, because on first reading, all you have is the poem. While this might be a problem in a more referential literary form in the space of the poem, this openness to interpretation becomes a generous, and generative, thing. The sonically inclined might read the poem and enjoy the manner in which *out, pot,* and *lot* chime together;

for the narrative obsessive there is the matter of who the old man is, why he ran and where from; and for some readers the visual image will spring to mind making the poem into a kind of photograph.

While some homages to visual art might place the poem as a post hoc explication of an image, the poems collected here carry their own sensation *as poems*. Yes, that sensation is drawn from works of visual art, but one needn't view those works to enjoy these poems. Indeed it was a particular thrill on first reading the collection to imagine the artworks. What is to say an imagined artwork is not also important? Are we not all engaged in a fictionalizing process when we apprehend an artwork, creating a context for it in our heads?

These questions are at the heart of *The Art Poems*. Even the title invites us to view the poems in a different light (it put me in mind of how music becomes *sound art* when it veers too close to noise). What is an art poem? What can a poem add to the field of art criticism? Amanda Bintu Holiday is well-placed to answer such questions given that she has been a practicing artist for many years, and has in that time presented art in a number of mediums and cultural landscapes. This sense of versatility as an artist lends the collection a pleasing variety of textures.

One of the most exciting aspects of Holiday's style is the sharpness of her wit. I found myself smiling often while reading these poems and imagining the poems being spoken. Two especially brilliant examples of Holiday's gift are the poems "Hat" and "The Angel," which, in the ways they employ an everyday kind of surrealism, serve to show us the absurdities that come to light when you turn something on its head (or, in the case of "Hat," when you wear it on your head):

> "It's not a hat," the girl
> hissed, rushing to my side,
> about to snatch the handbag from my head.
> Her colleague smirked, then stopped.

Both read thunder in my eyes.

"It is now," I insisted,
and handed her my card.
"I'd like to wear it out."

While the scene depicted here could be thought of as merely humorous, it also encourages a sense of ownership over one's particular vantage point. The poem and the collection seem to be saying that this too is a valid way of seeing. This collection is brimming with such affirmations, and it repays a careful reader who leans in to hear the beguiling voices in which these poems speak.

IN THE HOUSE OF MY FATHER

My father lived
in a skin house,
four flaking walls
pinned together
in the palm of a hand.

My father prayed
everyday
that the pins would hold,
that skin was enough
to stop the wind blowing in,
and our family blowing out.

WIND

She had learned to rise from the dead;
dip and hover around
the bereaved
disguised in finery;
a batik burqua
lifted on the wind;
a listening presence
in gardens, in the park;
eavesdropping
on the griefs
soaking out a life.

TRACE

Inside
the Tokoloshe had punctured herself
on a door handle
and struggled awhile,
limbs flailing upside,
trapped against glass,
a headless blot.

Outside,
two sisters stared in
hands pressed against the glass,
mouthing shapes,
helpless.

THE DAME WITH THE GOAT'S FOOT

The two-stringed banjo plays
a theme to our aging. Old soaks,
we sit and talk out the weather,
our fortunes and the price of youth.

We sit in worn frills and garters,
holding on to our daughters
and granddaughters
who sleep, unhampered
by our laments,
our songs of love and folly

of men who carried us away
on the back of goats.
To dance in castles
and dine on lizards and mint tea.

How we, in our prime,
bold in baubles and bustiers,
did battle with taxidermists,
tax collectors,
and our husbands.

THE BLUE POT

How the old man ran
with his belly out
and a spindly cane
and a big blue pot
pressed on his head
and his barky dog
atop the lot.

HAT

I fondled the soft white leather,
tried all the zips,
tossed away yellow tissue inside
and rummaged in the pockets.

The assistant cleared her throat.
Her colleague rolled her eyes.
"That's 1,800 dollars," she confirmed,
annoyed.

Stood before the mirror,
I slowly turned around
and slipped it on my head.
Yo!

"It's not a hat," the girl
hissed, rushing to my side,
about to snatch the handbag from my head.
Her colleague smirked, then stopped.
Both read thunder in my eyes.

"It is now," I insisted,
and handed her my card.
"I'd like to wear it out."

THE ANGEL

The donkey was stubborn
and Mary dug her heels into its side.
But the mule was tired of walking
and now the baby was crying;
fat little baby all swaddled
and plumpy, and Mary
jiggled him and tickled him
and put him to her breast.
And still he was teary
and Joseph had walked
off to lay a brick wall
and have his hair styled
into a flick. *Goddamnit. Men.*
But Mary bit her tongue
and sent a quiet
prayer up to the sky;
Someone come and help!
And the angel swooped
down almost straight away
and at first there was a
tussle. Mary held on.
He's just a few weeks old,
don't take him to heaven yet.
And the angel, calm and firm,
said she'd take the baby
to the Pyramids to see the Pope
and maybe some art—
then bring him back.
And Mary was relieved she'd

see her son again and
thanked the winged lady
before she trotted on.

THE END

Death came
with cockroaches
and sticky flies
in three tall letters:
doubled-eyed,
one-eyed,
and blind.
Tough henchmen
slitting sex
with a sword,
a thick penis,
and a skull.
Gatekeepers of
the shacks,
slaking lust
and thirst with
a toxic stain.

Hamba kahle.

CROSS

We all have a cross to bear,
a thick sleeper—burnt wood
(borne across the shoulder back
with fortitude, resolve, impatience)
that wears down hard. We hitch and tilt
this way, that,
cursing our load, plotting
secretly to ditch the blunted beam
in some passing alley or well

where God won't look.

LOSS OF VIRGINITY

And afterwards she lay on the hilltop
motionless and cool,
staring at the sky wondering
what was expected now.

He had muttered expletives
into her hair
throughout as he thrust away.

He smelt of bracken.
The blood ran. He handed her a flower
then stood up, and villagers
below the ridge cheered,
and they all walked away
back through the fields.

The yellow fox came
and sat on her neck
until they had all gone.

RASHA AND AGOSTA

Long ago, in Madagascar, when Rasha was four,
a purple snake slithered past her foot,
in and out of the light,
and she picked it up and flicked it through the air,
round and round her head, delighted until
Nan-nan had come running out shrieking
and snatched the deadly reptile
from her plump fist and pounded it into the ground.

Later, Nan-nan apologized
and taught her a trick which changed Rasha's life.
Nan-nan made her watch a serpent coil and
slide out switchback on its belly,
then Nan rolled up her tongue and blew out
a strange hollow whistle and slit her eyes,
and stared and stared ahead, until
the sinewed snake lifted slowly up
from the ground, rapt in dance.

And that is what Rasha learned to do:
charm snakes and make them dance.
She joined the circus and toured the world
and danced with snakes for money.
She whipped snakes and flicked them
over and under her thighs, then
draped them round her neck in heavy coils
of pendant python.

And one day Agosta came,
this pigeon-chested Frenchman with
lips so puckered up to kiss
that the very first time they met,
Rasha leaned in and planted
a soft smacker right upon
his birdy bouche to his surprise.
He'd never been close-up to black
lips before. He was hooked.
They fell in love unconditionally
and got married in the Circus tent—
he splendid in epaulettes,
his corporal chest puffed out,
and she with her best snake—
hung across her shoulders.
And they have stayed together
happily, ever since.

THE CRABS

The sea had been flat and still, barely lapping,
and lulled by heat and rum;
we lay back in the boats drifting,
damp handkerchiefs on our faces
against the sun.

And before long,
one by one, *badoom, badoom,*
our pirogues thudded up on sand and pebbles,
wedging us askew on the shore.
Big Paul woke first and leapt out
shouting, "Santos Caranguejos!"
Monster crabs; pink, ungainly,
blinked back slowly and waved their claws.

We grabbed oars and ran
at the crustaceans, poking fleshy faces,
beating hardened shells,
driving them inland. Yet more came—
an army sideways from the sea.
Soon we were surrounded:
flushed, hard-bodied hordes.

Paul ordered us, "Pare!" Lay down our sticks.
We dragged our boats to
the ocean edge, and as we waited
for the moon tide and staved
off hunger, we sang songs
to the fickle creatures, who now
danced in lines across the sand.

When midnight came, we loaded up
and set sail.

TESTIMONY WITH EMPTY HANDS
(with homage to G G Marquez)

Our mother's blood
seeped down the street
from where she was stabbed
eleven times through the heart

down the gutters
to our school
and under the door
and into the room
where we sat
at our desks
empty handed
reaching for answers.

WAR

Even now, the fighters
clumped together
and soaked in blood
shouted *War,*
and *War* again, and shook
fists at the heavens
where angels, timid and fluttery,
hid in the clouds.

And in her grave,
the bull wife
turned over and screamed,
"No more!"

But no one heard
and it was already too late.
Culled bodies
clogged the highway
soon to join her.

MUSE

She was the model,
the muse, a conduit
posed to draw out
a linear moment,
a mirage
by holding a mirror
up to the goatman
(who was Paulo;
who was the Minotaur;
who was huffy and vain
and smelt of meat
and unkindness)
just so he could grimace
at himself or at her
or at Picasso,
who drew sharp
and quick
like a hunter
skinning flesh from
a hare with
each pencil stroke,
til the paper
was tossed on the floor
and they sneaked
a look, and were
thrilled again by the grace
of fine lines and magic
they had extorted.

EARTH

Squatters
on earth's big ball
dig and piss
and plant the seed.
There is no rent to pay
to fuck and fight
and love and bleed
or fake the stock
sky high
for what?

AMBASSADOR

The ambassador (to Guinea Bissau)
likes to chill.

Sometimes she'll sit
in stonewashed jeans,
take off her wig (ooh the itch)
and that bloody mink,

and suck on
a Cuban cigar
in her bra.

HOLE

He was gone
down the dark hole.
We reached out,
we cried,
we hollered,
we looked,
we peered in
down and down
into black
char soot
tunnel
infinitum.

Stretched hands
pulled us
back as,

unknown,
his shed self,
white light,
headless,
joined in us.

ACKNOWLEDGMENTS

"In the House of my Father" after Donald Rodney's photograph
In the House of my Father
"Wind" after Yinka Shonibare (MBE)'s sculpture *Wind Sculpture*
"Trace" after Virginia Chihota's screen print *Untitled*
"The Dame with the Goat's Foot" after Paula Rego's painting
The Dame with the Goat's Foot
"The Blue Pot" after Bill Traylor's artwork *Untitled*
"Hat" after Zanele Muholi's photograph *Babhekile II*
"The Angel" after Paula Rego's painting *On the way to Egypt*
"The End" after Billy Mandindi's lino cut *Untitled*
"Cross" after Paula Rego's aquatint *Untitled*
"Loss of Virginity" after Paul Gauguin's painting *The Loss of
Virginity*
"Rasha and Agosta" after Christian Schad's painting *Agosta, the
Pigeon-Chested Man, and Rasha, the Black Dove*
"The Crabs" after unknown etching *Shipwrecked Portuguese sol-
diers battle giant crabs in the Indian ocean 1601*
"Testimony with empty hands" after Virginia Chihota's screen
print *Testimony with empty hands*
"War" after Sante Scaldaferri's painting *Untitled*
"Muse" after Picasso's etching *Girl Helping Minotaur*
"Ambassador" after Lynette Yiadom Boakye's painting *Ambassador*
"Hole" after Belkis Ayón's collograph *Untitled*